LEARN TO DRAW
ANGRY BIRDS™
SPACE

ROVIO BOOKS

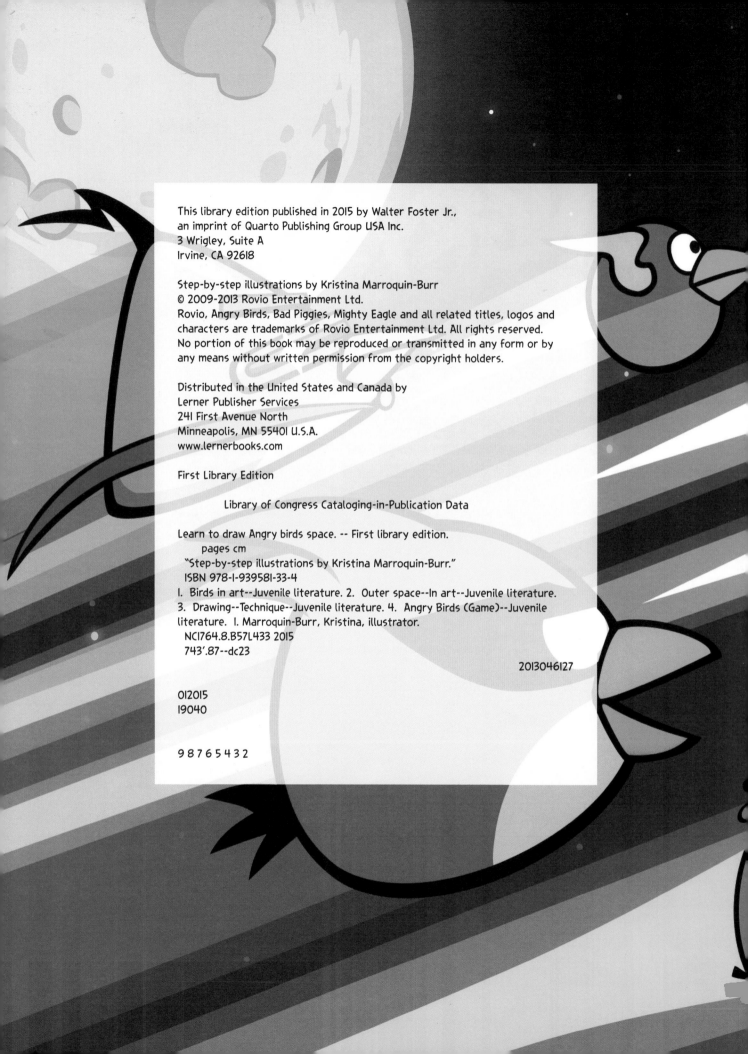

This library edition published in 2015 by Walter Foster Jr.,
an imprint of Quarto Publishing Group USA Inc.
3 Wrigley, Suite A
Irvine, CA 92618

Step-by-step illustrations by Kristina Marroquin-Burr
© 2009-2013 Rovio Entertainment Ltd.
Rovio, Angry Birds, Bad Piggies, Mighty Eagle and all related titles, logos and
characters are trademarks of Rovio Entertainment Ltd. All rights reserved.
No portion of this book may be reproduced or transmitted in any form or by
any means without written permission from the copyright holders.

Distributed in the United States and Canada by
Lerner Publisher Services
241 First Avenue North
Minneapolis, MN 55401 U.S.A.
www.lernerbooks.com

First Library Edition

Library of Congress Cataloging-in-Publication Data

Learn to draw Angry birds space. -- First library edition.
    pages cm
  "Step-by-step illustrations by Kristina Marroquin-Burr."
  ISBN 978-1-939581-33-4
1. Birds in art--Juvenile literature. 2. Outer space--In art--Juvenile literature.
3. Drawing--Technique--Juvenile literature. 4. Angry Birds (Game)--Juvenile
literature. I. Marroquin-Burr, Kristina, illustrator.
  NC1764.8.B57L433 2015
  743'.87--dc23

2013046127

012015
19040

9 8 7 6 5 4 3 2

TABLE OF CONTENTS

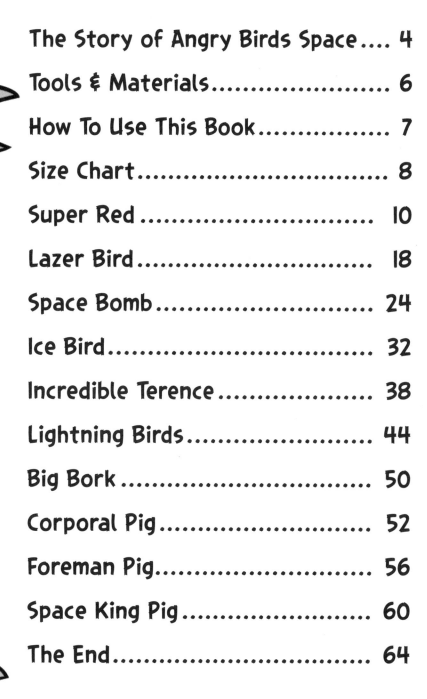

THE STORY OF ANGRY BIRDS SPACE

IN SPACE, NO ONE CAN HEAR YOU OINK!

The Angry Birds have always guarded their precious eggs against the attacks of the egg-hunting Bad Piggies, but one day a totally new menace appears on Piggy Island.

A huge wormhole opens in the sky and a bird resembling an ice cube storms through the hole. It is the Ice Bird, and he is trying to protect his Eggsteroid—a magic egg-shaped asteroid. Soon a huge metallic arm reaches out from the wormhole, and everyone on the island hears the booming evil laughter of the Space Pigs.

The Space Pigs scoop up both the Eggsteroid and the Eggs into the looming darkness. The birds immediately rush after their eggs, flinging themselves into the wormhole just before it disappears. Suddenly, the Angry Birds find themselves in a strange space universe! Their appearance has changed and they are geared up like superheroes. Before realizing what happened, they see their enemy with their eggs! Can you guess what they did next?

TOOLS & MATERIALS

Before you begin drawing, you need to gather the right tools. Start with a regular pencil, an eraser, and a pencil sharpener. When you're finished with your drawing, you can bring your characters to life by adding color with crayons, colored pencils, markers, or even paint!

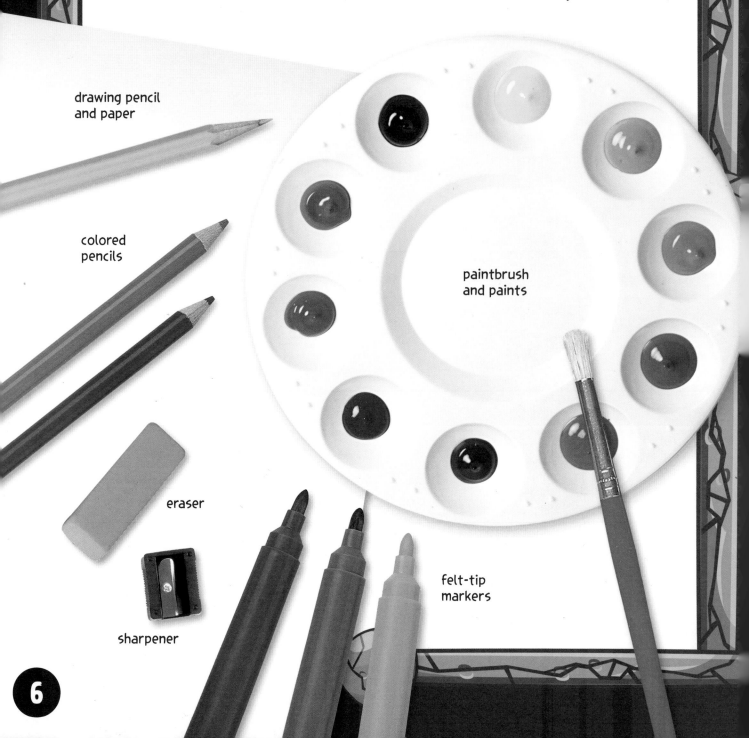

drawing pencil and paper

colored pencils

paintbrush and paints

eraser

felt-tip markers

sharpener

HOW TO USE THIS BOOK

Professional artists draw characters in steps. The key is to start with simple shapes and gradually add the details. The blue lines will help guide you through the process.

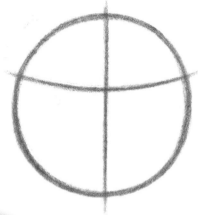

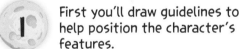

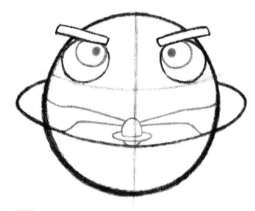

1 First you'll draw guidelines to help position the character's features.

2 Next you'll add the details, step by step.

3 When you finish adding the details, erase your guidelines. Then darken your final sketch lines with a pen or a marker.

SIZE CHART

Super Red   Lightning Birds   Lazer Bird

Corporal Pig   Foreman Pig   King Pig

Space Bomb

Ice Bird

Incredible Terence

Big Bork

SUPER RED

Super Red is the leader of the Space Flock. He trusts in his *SuperSpace Mask,* which has multiple features from tracking devices to a super-zoom. Red will not rest until he finds the missing eggs.

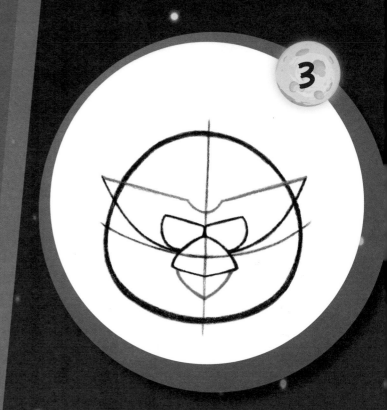

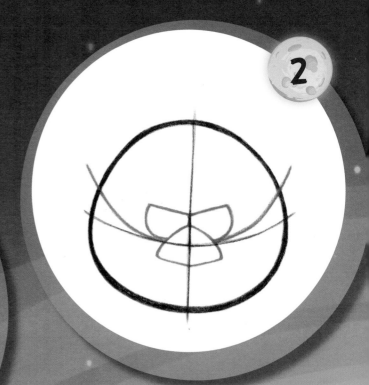

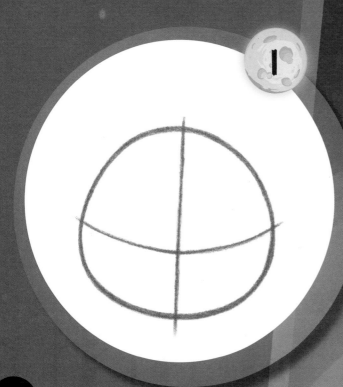

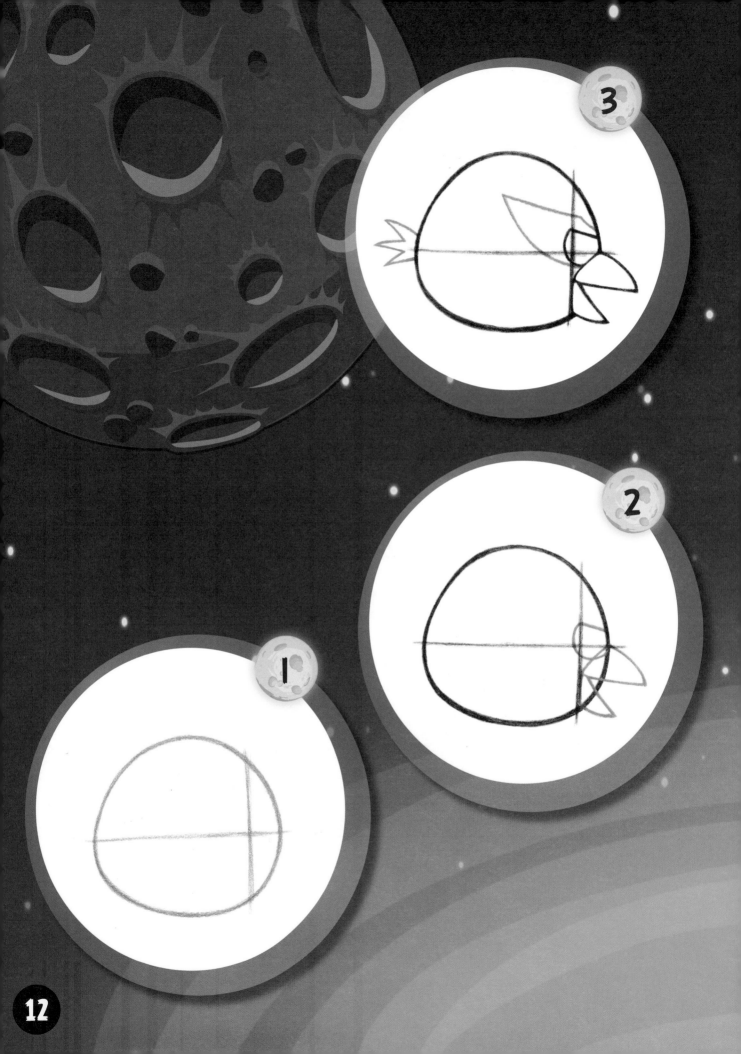

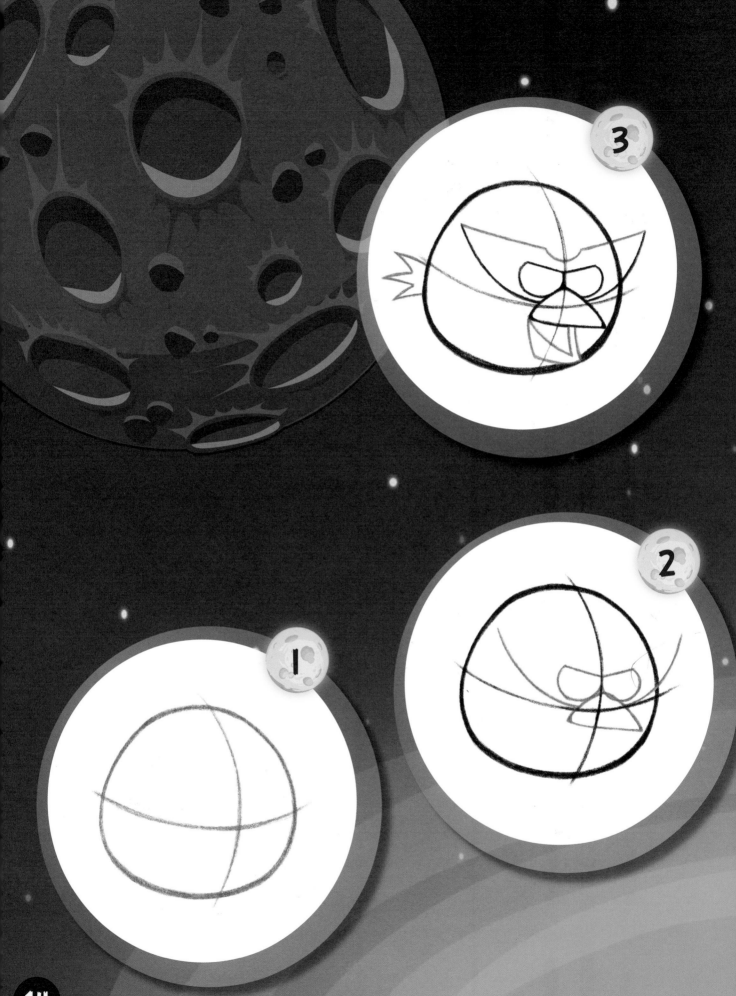

SUPER RED'S EXPRESSIONS

Screaming

Colliding

Cheering

Blinking

Flying

Looking Right

Jumping

17

LAZER BIRD

Lazer Bird is one of the fastest things in the universe when he uses his superpower, the *Ultimate Lazer Rush.* Lazer Bird is the joker of the group and, being a little impatient, he often gets the flock into trouble.

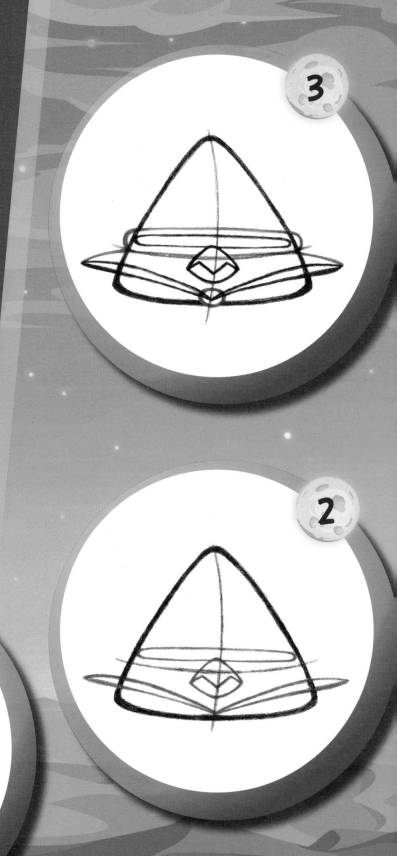

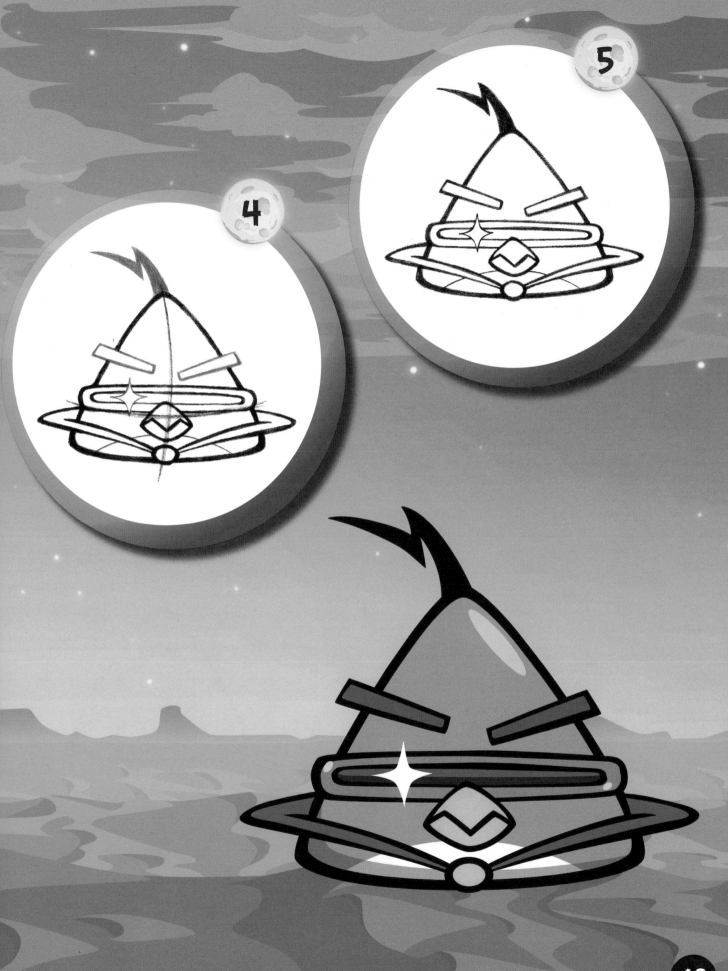

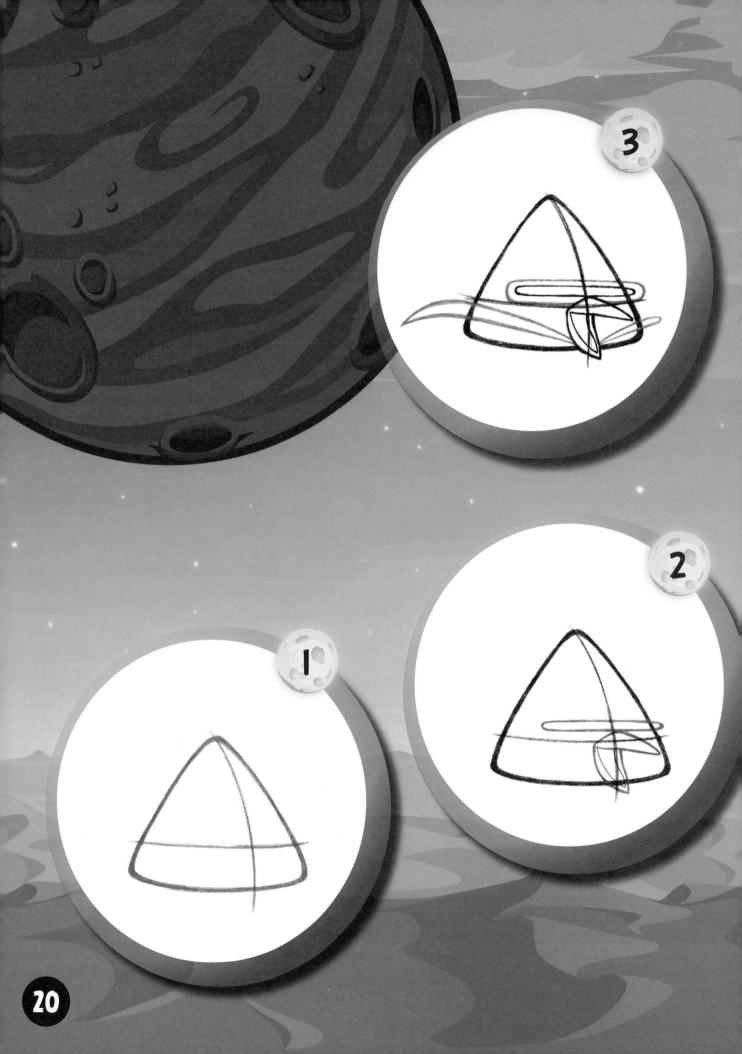

LAZER BIRD'S EXPRESSIONS

Colliding

Screaming

Looking Right

Blinking

Cheering

Jumping

SPACE BOMB

Space Bomb wears a superhero cape with a shining Angry Birds Egg Brooch attached to it. He loves using his superpower, *Shock Bang,* which destroys unwanted objects and sends them to outer space.

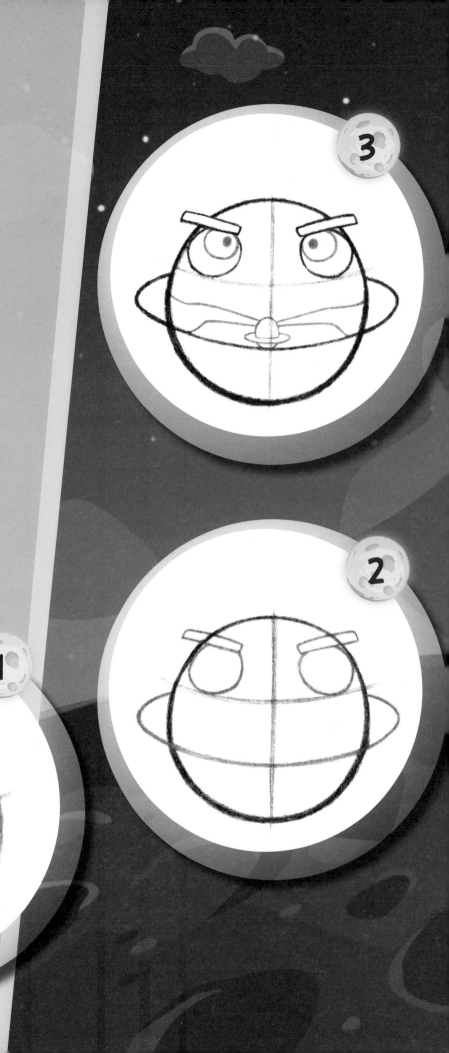

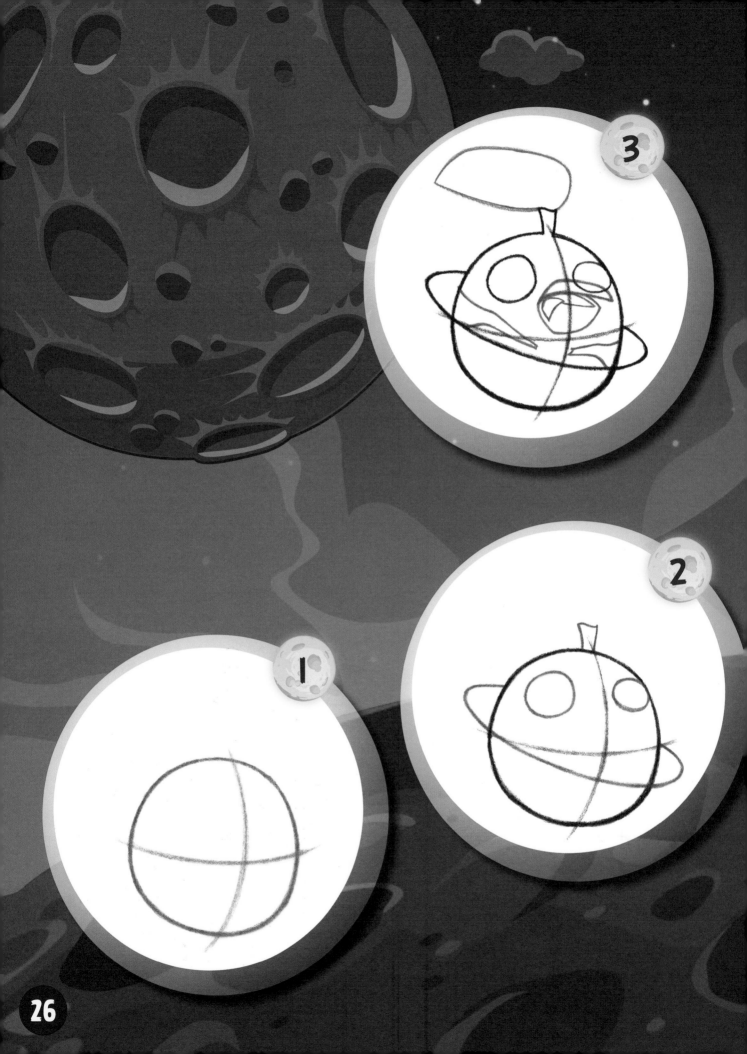

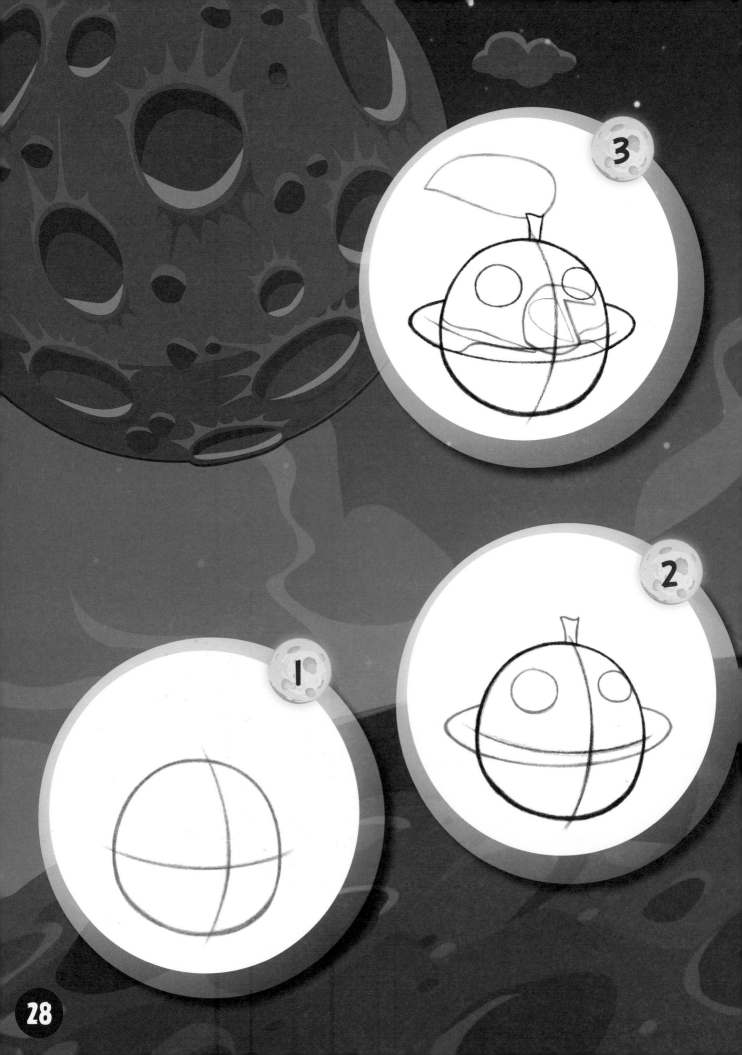

Screaming

Colliding

Blinking

Looking Right

Cheering

Blowing Up

ICE BIRD

Ice Bird is the coolest of the birds. His super-power, *Deep Freeze Attack,* turns different elements into ice. With icicles for a plume and tail, he has the appearance of an ice cube. The Angry Birds are helping Ice Bird to get his Eggsteroid back from the Space Pigs.

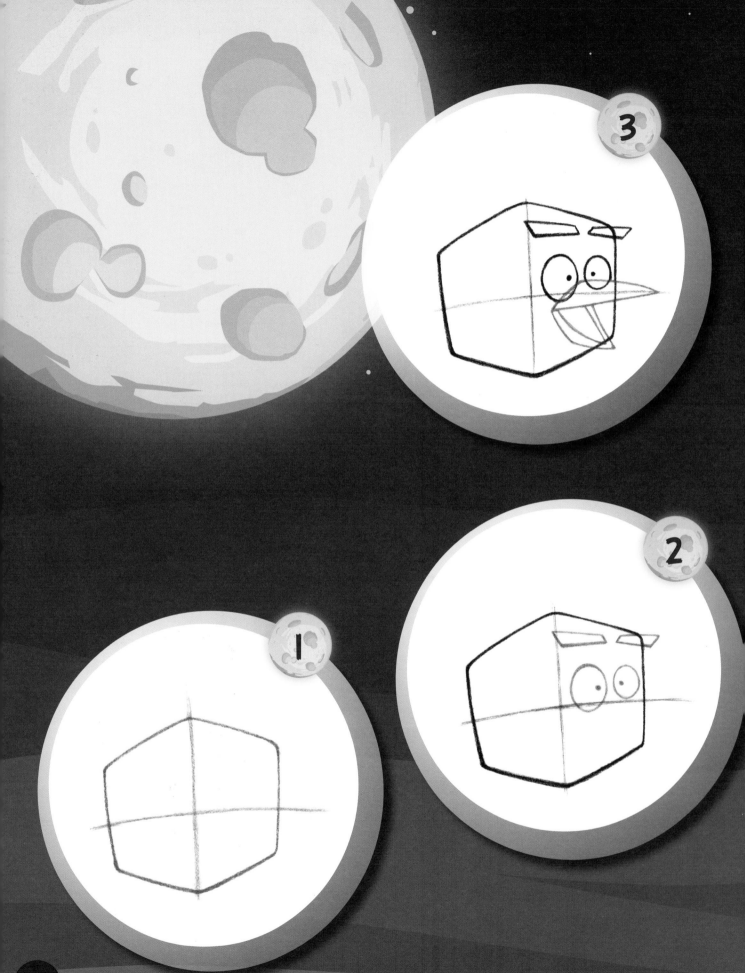

ICE BIRD'S EXPRESSIONS

Screaming

Colliding

Blowing Up

Blinking

Flying

Looking Right

Cheering

37

INCREDIBLE TERENCE

Even though Incredible Terence is bright green, he should never be confused with the pigs or he will get very angry! This silent and enigmatic bird hero always has his *Incredible Monster Crush* superpower turned on.

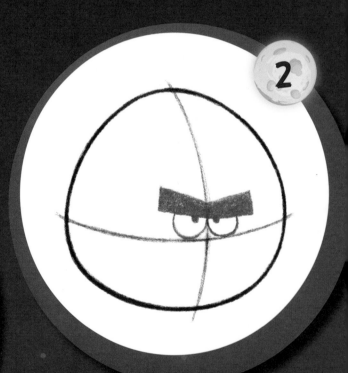

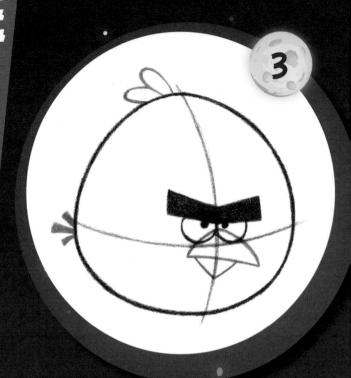

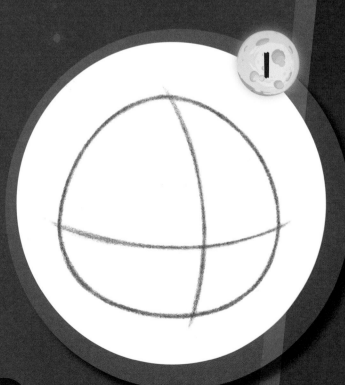

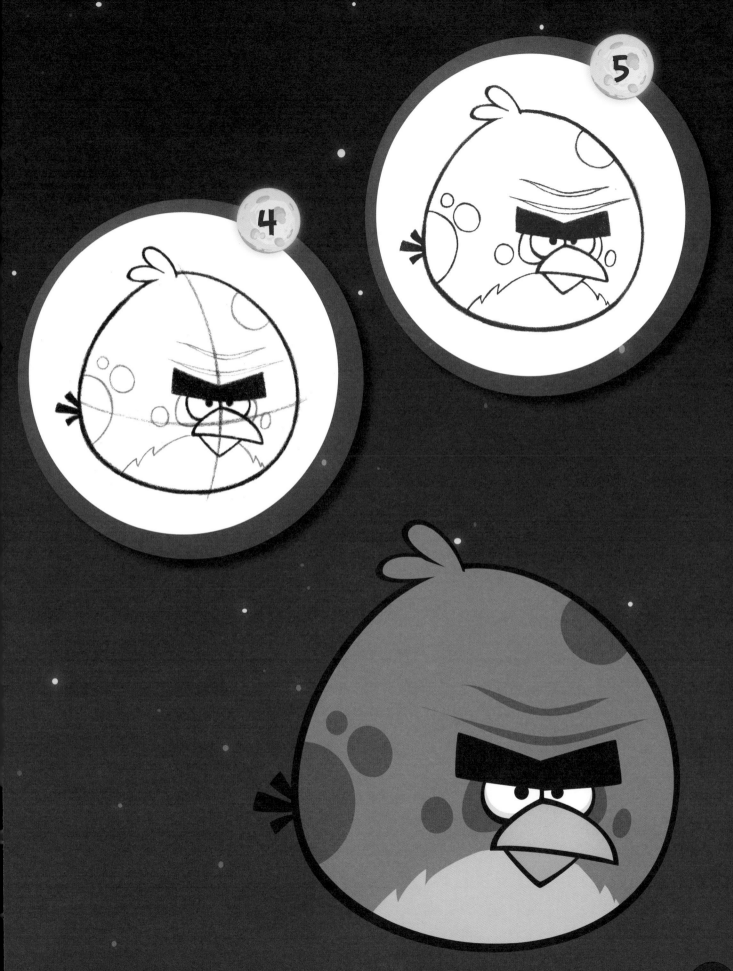

Screaming

Looking Left

Cheering

Blinking

Flying

Jumping

Looking Right

LIGHTNING BIRDS

The Lightning Birds travel in a pack of three. They are adventurers whose curiosity and liveliness drive the birds as they face new challenges. Their superpower, the *Triple Vaporizer*, comes in handy in the freezing hollowness of space.

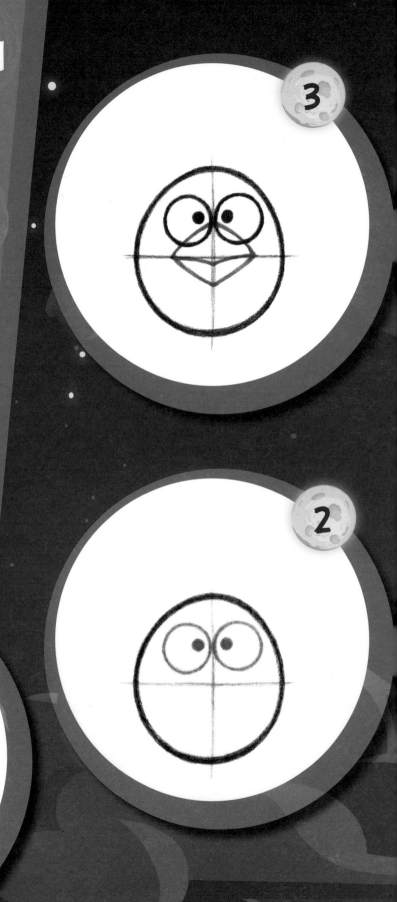

Colliding

Screaming

Blinking

Cheering

Flying

Jumping

Looking Right

49

BIG BORK

This Space Pig has large green spots on his skin and facial features that are too small for his huge head—he's simply MASSIVE! But that's pretty much the scariest thing about him. Generally kind and harmless, Big Bork only frightens others because of his size.

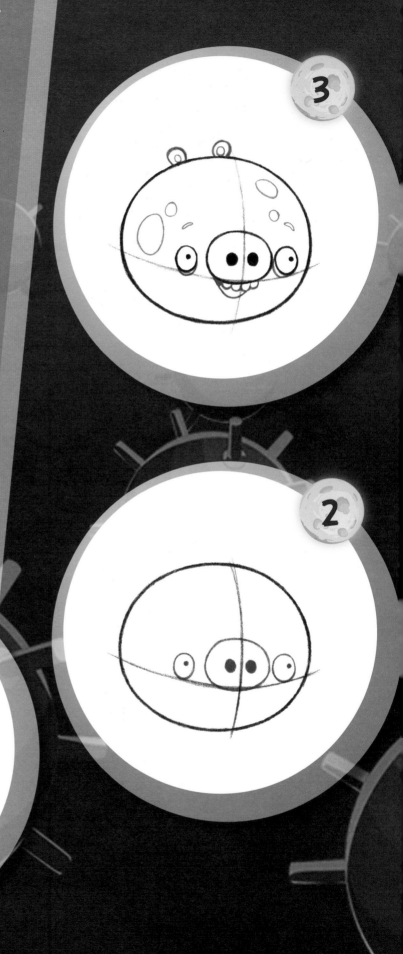

CORPORAL PIG

As commander of the Space Pig army, the Corporal Pig wears a shiny, metal antenna attached to his steel helmet. However, this leader is not to be messed with; he's known for being a bully who rules with an iron fist!

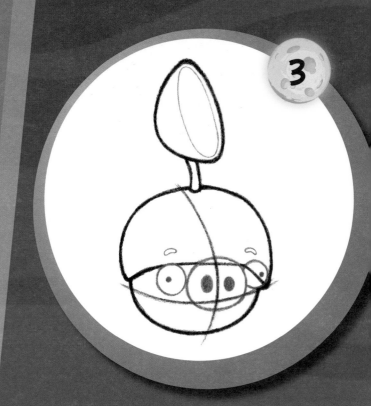

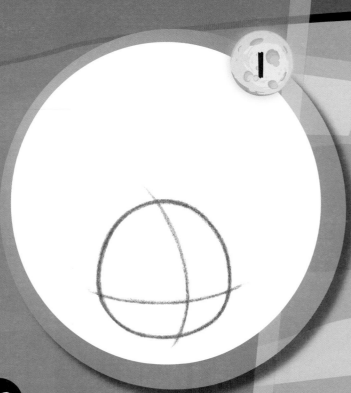

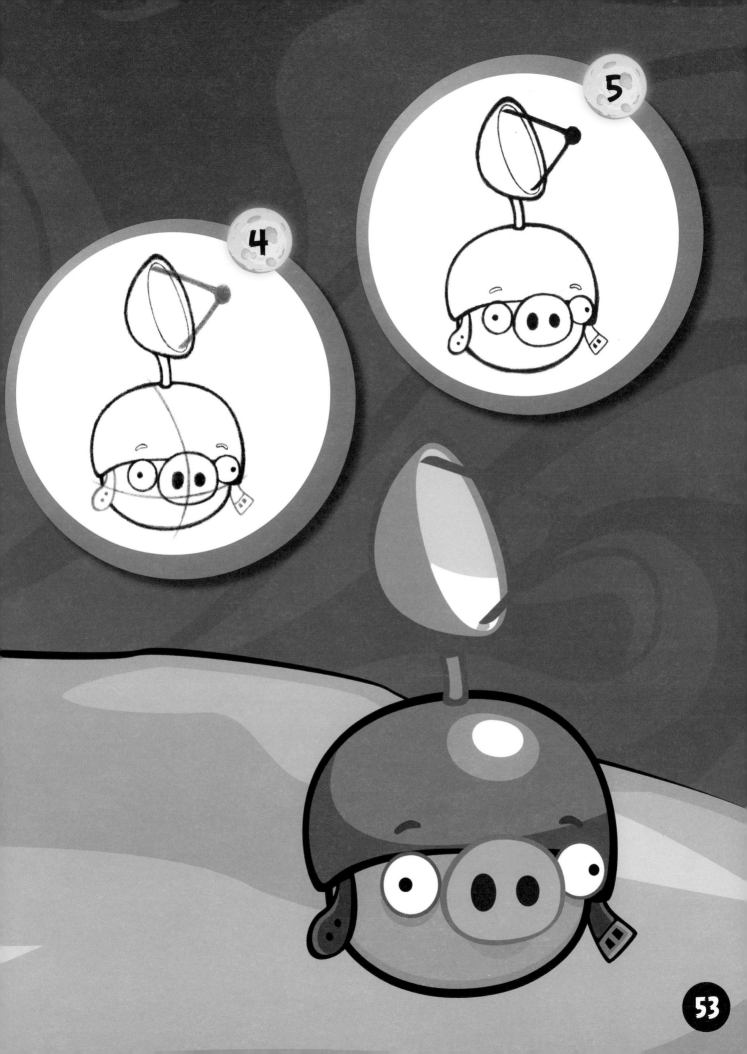

FOREMAN PIG

The Foreman Pig manages the building of contraptions and structures, and considers himself the ultimate expert—though nobody else agrees. He's usually grumpy, and can often be heard muttering to himself that life was better back in the old days.

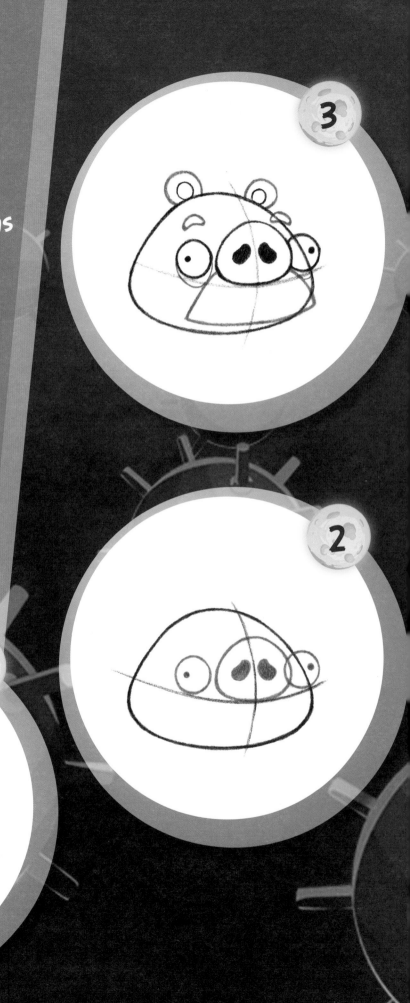

Kids these days...

SPACE KING PIG

In Space, the King Pig often adapts his choice of headgear and signature gold, jewel-encrusted crown to the climate and scenery. Though he is the ruler of all pigs, he is known for being lazy and immature.

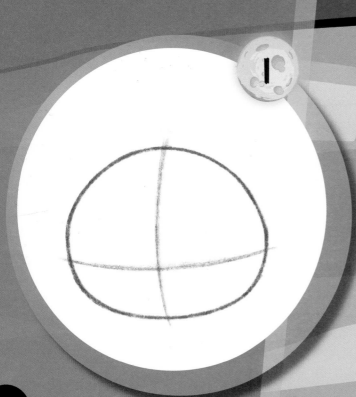

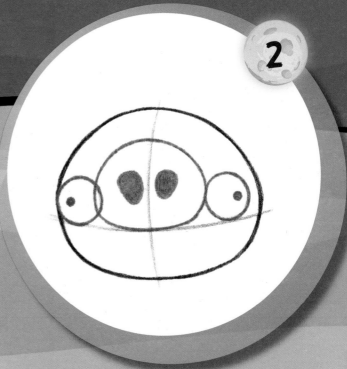

THE END

Now that you've learned the secrets to drawing the superhero Angry Birds and Space Pigs, create your own out-of-this-world adventures—without ever leaving planet Earth! All you need is a pencil, paper, and your own imagination!